I0210485

# Tapestry of Counterpoint

*poems by*

# Rosanne Osborne

*Finishing Line Press*
Georgetown, Kentucky

# Tapestry of Counterpoint

The world has to exist in counterpoint…You have a melody or a tune. And it's beautiful. And then you have another melody or a tune, and another one. And you put them all together and play them simultaneously, like singing "Row, Row, Row Your Boat" in canon. And instead of each individual melody losing anything by being combined as a whole, it becomes like a wonderful tapestry, a tapestry where each of these individual threads doesn't lose its meaning, doesn't lose its identity, doesn't lose its own *raison d'etre*, its own reason for being, but contributes to the whole tapestry of counterpoint….
—Mohammed Fairouz, *On Being*. April 15, 2015

Copyright © 2023 by Rosanne Osborne
ISBN 979-8-88838-357-5  First Edition
All rights reserved under International and Pan-American Copyright Conventions.
No part of this book may be reproduced in any manner whatsoever without written
permission from the publisher, except in the case of brief quotations embodied in
critical articles and reviews.

## ACKNOWLEDGMENTS

Many thanks to the editors of the following journals in which some of these
poems appeared:

"Maneuvers," *The Louisville Review*, Fall 2022
"Before We Knew," *Everyday Poems*, June 19, 2012
"Complicity," *Ruminate*, Summer 2009
"The Ground of Being," *The Christian Century*, September 15, 2007

Publisher: Leah Huete de Maines
Editor: Christen Kincaid
Author Photo: Rosanne Osborne
Cover Design: Elizabeth Maines McCleavy


Order online: www.finishinglinepress.com
also available on amazon.com

Author inquiries and mail orders:
Finishing Line Press
PO Box 1626
Georgetown, Kentucky 40324
USA

# Table of Contents

## Tolkien in the Somme

Mouse and man share the interruption
of war. Tiny claws graze knuckles
accustomed to grasping the nib's holder.
Neither understands the shudder
of the land beneath their twin souls,
a circumstance at once alien
yet somehow woven into their kind.

What must the mouse think of this man
lying in the deep trench of what was
his field, daring to intrude on his terrain?
The flesh, so soft, so warm, bids
comparison to the hard crust of steel
the hand steadies in a trembling world.
Breathlessly, time faults.

Seeds burst in the minds of both,
shadows of another reality beyond
the smoke, the destruction of the wild.
The mouse-mind shapes its kernel
of golden corn, restores gastronomic
memory of fullness, believing
harvest to be reality beyond dream.

The man-mind processes the lightness
of furred touch, marvels at a connection
frozen in time. Beneath its folds
and layers, the cerebral cortex quivers
with the faint glow of a dragon's eye
yet to be shaped in the imaginary
tread of silence in a mountain lair.

## Making the Immaterial Material

> *But my soul-spot bright.*
> —David Mitchell, *The Bone Clocks*

It's a neat trick, Mitchell, if you
      can do it.

Locating the opening to the soul
      in one spot

on the body surface like a gaping
      mouth

or a blowhole on a humpback
      spine,

an ear that hears harmonies
      honed

by waves rebellious in moon-ordered
      time.

## We Never Know

*Why at the beginning of things is there always light?*
    –Richard Flanagan, *The Narrow Road to the Deep North*

The foal, all knobby knees and spindly legs, struggled
    to gain a hoof-hold on the world of light.

His wet-sack body glistened in the Sunday sun
    as he tottered to the mother's milk he knew
somehow where to find. I was transfigured by first
    birth and the miracle in my transformed eyes.

All hope seemed to rest in the star in that sorrel forehead,
    above the white-stockinged feet. I had no way
of knowing then of the coyote's slashing teeth, the leg
    snapped like a brittle stick to fuel a fire,
or the trader's truck that would do little to sop debt.
    We never know, do we? That light darkens.

The dawn over a dreaming stone-dominant village
    is made deceptive by the stealth of incoming
missile fire, the child mangled beneath the rubble
    of morning table, a crust falling from severed
fingers. No one knows darkness will cover dawn.

Or think of the early morning light that beams
    from the mother's eye, hurrying her
children into a stranger's truck, imagining the end
    of freedom's trek to a waiting, welcoming
world, willing her mind against the what-ifs
    of misfortune, false rumors, and loneliness.

Children and light, the inseparable alchemy
    of hope has its roots so deeply entangled
in the web-work of the foundation of our souls
    that we can be no other than newly born.

Ours is the waking at first light, the thrust of birth
beyond the womb of darkness.

## Preaching the Shine

*Soul-polishing was the family business.*
*–Niall Williams, History of the Rain*

So, that was what was wanted
when the preacher asked us
to open the doors of our hearts.

With that big white handkerchief
used to mop sweat from his brow,
the church growing hot and steamy

as the revival rose to its climax,
he intended to reach right inside
and give our sinful souls a snap

of the old polishing rag, matching
the shoeshine that my father paid
two bits for at the barbershop.

## The Ground of Being

The artist's eye caught
the bent iron grating
intended to separate the living
from the dead, the bars
pulled apart
as though a wandering
specter had recovered
his human form, escaped
a deadened community.

The camera lens focused
the rows of tampered vaults,
doors nearly askew, lines
of dead diminishing
to infinity.

Framed by pillars past,
the photo pressed into time
absence of brass bands blowing
funereal dirges,
colorful umbrellas swaying
to the beat, second-liners
celebrating release.

I thought of reading
old Creole stories
of George Washington Cable
and Grace King, the scourge
of yellow fever, the cycle
of death and renewal
acted out in another century.

Or my own mental death
and renewal in the sixties.
Coming to New Orleans
as a religious zealot,

a fundamentalist devotee
from the heartland, I remembered
the damp breeze blowing

across the iron bed frame
where I lay reading Paul Tillich
one Saturday afternoon.

His text called into question
all that Pleasant Bethel Baptist Church
had taught me, my literal faith tested
by questions I had never allowed
to take root, Noah's flood, the sacrificial
testing of Abraham, the proposition
that Esther would become queen
by offering her body. My mind
embraced the freedom of doubt.

Driving past Lafayette Cemetery
to seminary classes, I pondered
the rationale for burying the dead
above the ground, the belief
that levees would hold, the cockeyed
certainty that the mystical combination
of voodoo and faith would somehow
render the Big Easy indomitable.

Katrina changed all that, but
New Orleans has always shunted
bones to the rear, reopened
tombs for the newly dead, believed
in resurrection.

## Third Grade

*Think of it as my own personal Schrödinger's cat.*
  *–Karen Joy Fowler, We Are All Completely Beside Ourselves*

*Is this your father?*
My teacher opened
the morning paper
before my eyes.

I recognized the red
and black checks,
sleeves carefully rolled
above the grey sweatshirt.

The angry grimace
fastened on the mangled
slot machine seemed
to belong to some other
daughter's father.

The image haunted
arithmetic, clouded
the words of a story
problem, loitered
like the fugitive ache
of a worrisome molar.

Meaning, an evasive
life-conundrum,
its clues buried
with Schrödinger's cat
in a white birch box
in Chilhowee's cemetery.

## Ode to Drawers that Fail to Close

The delicate balance between
drawers and dresser contains
the personality of the bedroom
piece. Whether it's called bureau,
commode, highboy, or simply
a chest of drawers, its disposition
is destined by the tongue in groove
of the fit of drawers to cabinet.

Drawers ajar, strangely angled,
calls for assistance shouted
from the ill-fitted oak mark
the lack of created skill. Sired
by uncertain hands, the tongue
lolls loosely out of the mouth
of the imbecilic wood. Socks
are destined to peep beneath
the folds of speech. Their obscene
toes lick their cornered chops.

Foot in mouth teeters dangerously
between decorum and decadence
in the corner of the room. It bids
me enter an ill-fitted world where
who I am and what is wanted
never matches. Argyles and stripes
seek a destiny where only silken
solids are allowed. Woolen threads
are coarse and scratch the surface
in ways the feet can never hide.

## Learning to Swim at 72

Beads of moisture cover ancient ligneous legs,
toes become timid talons gripping the sides
of a secure nest, stability of textured deck.

Frozen in time, 72 years transposes
skill-development, attempts childhood lessons,
trepidation floods my aged consciousness.

I cannot, will not, trust the authority
of my swimming teacher. Accustomed to control,
every recalcitrant nerve refuses capitulation.

The aquamarine clarity of water reflects
my foreboding. The wavering lines at the bottom
of the pool are bars incarcerating

the paralyzed bend of arthritic limbs, smothering
my mind, my ambition to dive as a youthful
swimmer, thrusting my body into the deep

certainty of buoyancy. I remember
the struggle and release that came
with my first hesitant strokes away

from the pool's perimeter, my first agonizingly slow
lap toward bodily freedom in a substance alien
to my nature. Yet my terror will not allow

me to duplicate the release incarnating those virgin
attempts to swim. Poised between debacle
and conquest, I stop thinking, feeling–

deny all that has gone before and all that will follow.
In nothingness, I give myself to the splash
of a prime bellyflop and sputter like a ten-year-old.

## Havarti in the Highest

Is it the way the word rolls off the tongue
that delights the senses even before
the cheese is chosen? I'll have Havarti,
I tell this deli sous chef, his knife poised
for a lasting imprint on the block
of buttery goodness about to climax
my roast beef sub. Danish
slices topping 100% purebred
American Angus, garnished with dark
brown English mustard. My taste buds
jealously watch the wheat roll warming
while my ears ring with "Havarti!"

## The Knell

I tripped down the broken sidewalks
past the vines choking shrubs once
trimmed, grass once mowed. Gyrated
broken steps and creaking porch
to push against the peeling paint
of the door where dream began.

The settling house refused to yield
its hold, but I was determined
to enter its drafty rooms, be where
dust and cobwebs illuminated
what seemed so easy to attain.
Feral cats scurried from stained

cushions of the sofa whose once
royal blue clung to my inner eye,
a partly knit sweater, tattered
yarn clinging to the needles,
Middlemarch its edges chewed
by daring rodents dreaming

of nests deep within the walls
where feline paws could never
reach. My mind swayed, hoofing
the discords of internal music,
the might-have-beens grooved
in the hoodwinking wainscot.

The house groaned and the door
left ajar shuddered in laughter
at the dumbshow within, the irony
of return. A long black snake
slithered soundlessly across the mantel,
mouthed an unsuspecting mouse.

## That Vaporing Apostle

Some accuse Paul of being smug
in his own suffering with all that talk
about things working for good.

> He preached a gospel of loss,
> a reductionist view of hoarding
> that Augustine admired.

If the man with three juicy Bartlett pears
drops one from the hole in his bag,
he will treasure the other two

> more completely. If the wind comes up
> and knocks the bag from his hand
> to the river below, he'll watch the pair

> > float away leaving the image of taste
> > in his mouth, desire on the bulbous
> > nerve endings that line his maw.

Will he be richer for his loss
as imagination pares the ruddy skin
holding the juice within the fruit?

**Yet**

I read Huck
the year I sat on the right side.
The room, reeking of sweeping compound
clinging to the runners lining our desks

and speckled trout swimming
in the oaks, October rain
beginning to fall
in the yard.

Jim's simple logic
that we all missed
sounded like the muffled adults
in Charlie Brown's Christmas

on the TVs
yet to be added to our homes,
yet to offer an alternative
to our imaginations.

**The Hunt**

Lanterns almost white
against the blackness of the night,
carbide hissing, igniting
the burn of youthful desire.
Boys like miners thread
their way through the dense
undergrowth, listening
to the distant bay of hounds.

Raccoons scurry from tree
to tree, testing the dense foliage.
Climbing high, they hear danger
in canine cries, and their hearts
beat against the sudden stillness
of the night. The forest sniffs
acetylene burning and knows
its vulnerability as boots

crackle across the leaf-laid pattern
of the flooring. The imminence
of death drips against the earth's
elements, and life trembles
as the dogs move in to tree
their prey. A rifle cracks and the thump
of furred life descends in the false light
of reflected lamps and panting boys.

## Silver Secrets

My computer allows me
to peer into an osprey nest
high above birches
in an Estonian forest.

Celebrating life, I remember
death. I see only my mother,
cold and lifeless at three a.m.,
in a hospital room across town.

The irony of time haunts
my enjoyment of the intimacy
of nature–a mother tending
her hatchlings–oblivious

to the miles that separate
watcher and watched, and I
wonder if she sees them, too.
How she loved driving

by the osprey nest high
above the road, straining
to see the bird she'd only seen
in pictures in her worn book.

Transported from Missouri
to Minnesota, she still marveled
that she had traveled, had
summered out of state.

And now, I can see what
she would have loved to have seen.
The unfairness of time's advance
causes me to look away, deny my gaze.

**Affinity**

With conviction I tipped the dirt
and the shovel's solid goodness
shot up my arm like a fuse fired.

For a second, the worn handle
gripped my fingers as though
I would not be released, a tongue

bonded to a metal pump in winter.
Gobsmacked, I looked at the bulbs
I meant to conceal in the rich loam

and they looked at me with the eyes
of the potatoes my parents planted
each March, a rustic Eucharist.

**Figs and Pomegranates**

Figs bursting from their skins,
      tart crunchy pomegranate seeds,
grapes succulent and fleshy,
        almonds and pistachio nuts,

tactile lusciousness a contrast
      to the aridity of the way
I have come, the desert of my mind.
        I slouched along,

a camel seeking cool water
      in the mirage of might be,
the semblance of ill-defined promise.
        My mask covering

the doppelgänger that threatens
      to eat its fill, stake its tent,
remain at daybreak
        to pile its stones.

## Rust

"You need a new wheelbarrow," my neighbor remarks
watching me trundle my shallow, rusting
cart to the curb, orphaned limbs and sticks
protruding like morning hair fresh
from an unmade bed. "I've a better one
that a friend brought for our yard sale."

I'm not impressed. He doesn't know that when
I lift the handles, the weight shifts
from my hands to those of my father sleeping
beneath the debris of a Missouri winter.
He doesn't know that this handcart
carries the fragments of my mind, the tributes

housed in the rubbish of winters turned
to spring, similes and metaphors waiting
the right poem, fractured lines
of hyperbole and hope, alliterative alleys
of childhood discards. How could he see
beyond rust, the sonnet reclaimed?

**Before We Knew**

Smoking was the old normal
of my childhood.
My mother's friends
lit their Camels between Cokes
on Saturdays at the local drug store.
My dad plowed the corn
with his Lucky Strikes
in his shirt pocket.

The crimson circle on the white
pack, the golden camel on hers
were images transferring
meaning to letters, my eyes
learning to read.

Her moon eclipsed his sun,
the ring of fire that held
them, comforted me
on darkened nights
curled to dream of
camels and pyramids
and the journey home
in our Studebaker sedan.

## Complicity

Spokes revolve, grind through the dusty track,
gravel pushed aside by neighbors' trucks

on the farm-to-market road that leads
to the field where my dad mows hay in scorching

sun, my handlebar basket cradling a Mason jar
of lemonade for him. On the road ahead

a long black snake. I freeze on wheels spinning dust,
watch it inch across the sun-baked clay, then slither

into the ditch. My dad mops sweat and swats flies
as he swills lemonade under the apple tree I climb

at the field's edge. I look down at the Ford tractor,
the long arm of the mowing blade that slices timothy

waiting to be baled, stored in the hayloft
where I hid last month, leaving my mother's

favorite cookie jar in pieces on the freshly
waxed floor. The glaze on sugar cookies

lingering on my tongue, I climb higher
in the old apple tree, shift to a limb that is certain

to bear my weight. Looking down, I study the remains
of a snake caught in the tines of the mower blade.

An apple ripens on the branch above my head.

## Stove Box Crib

My first days were spent in a shoebox
resting on the open door of an oven
in our family-run Blairstown restaurant.

I barely topped four pounds at birth
and lost to three before an old woman
from the country recommended goat

milk to ease me on into flesh.  Toothless,
hair tied down in a faded scarf, she
had urged fourteen to live, lost but three,

her stories of colic, whooping cough,
and measles threading air thick with
yesterday's cabbage, today's soup.

Bacon and eggs sizzled on the grill,
while my father flipped flap-jacks
and scraped hash browns to plates

warmed above my cardboard crib.
From the other side of the counter,
voices spoke of cattle lost to blackleg,

sheep attacked by coyotes, chickens
with coccidiosis. My grandmother
refilled coffee mugs chilling in hands

chapped by winter wind as stories
of fence line squabbles, burning barns,
and mortgage foreclosures sounded

to the strains of Roy Acuff's "Wabash
Cannonball" and I slept in a scrap
of blanket torn from mother's bed.

**Gathering**

*The sound of late childhood plays at our funerals.*
*–Richard Powers, Orfeo*

Concentration on the deceased, casket open
below the altar, is minimized, all but ignored,
as conversations waft about the evening wake.

Occasional eyes are cast that way, to be sure
the dead stay where they have been assigned,
no surprise stirring of resurrection. They prefer

the dead to know their place. Eyes averted,
folks huddle in the pews in forced talk
of the rain, the crops, family changes since

they last gathered. Then, not wanting to seem
too eager, they stray in two and threes toward
the kitchen, careful that the dead not realize

they came for the fried chicken, turnip greens
and cherry pie. They sidestep the plastic
face changelessly locked into its own take-home

box. Filling plates with potato salad, ham,
casseroled squash, and field peas fresh
from a fertile garden, death is deferred

to that other room, that sanctuary marked
by stiff life, fake makeup and careful hair,
the lingering fear of might have been.

## The Last Wash

The mashed potatoes always tasted of printer's ink
when I visited my grandparents, the printing press
in the dining room, the living room doubling
as the newspaper office. The two of them wrote
and printed *The Blairstown Record* each week,

she covering the news, he selling the ads.
Her fingers flew from case to setting stick,
right to left, upside down, her mirror
image copy locked line by line into the frame
that composed each page. He'd pull

the proof, his indelible pencil leaving purple
stains around his mouth as he checked her work.
I see him now, slumped under the green eyeshade
that allowed him to read through cataracts
forming on eyes that checked each edition while

she retired to the wash house to nudge their laundry
through the old ringer washer, to hoist the tubs,
to rinse and blue his starched white shirts. Later,
the neighbor noticed her legs, bent as though
she were sitting on the steps to rest, her head

pillowed on the concrete floor, the wash soaking
in the last tub. Dinah, her fat Boston Bull, sat
by her side. When my grandfather moved
to our house, he brought only the white shirts,
a single suit, and Dinah.

**Asperges**

When we country kids
went in town to school,
we were warned
to brush the hayseeds
from our hair.

Aspergillosis—
farmers lungs were ours.

Lusty, accustomed to ingesting
moldy hay, at home with cracked
grammar and homespun idioms,
we lacked the sapience the townies
took for granted.

We longed for
a priest to wave his aspergillum
above our heads, to aspirate
the barnyard mud
        from the soles
                of our brogans.

# Where Is My Grandmother's Davenport?

*"Road to Rebirth Diverges on a Mississippi Bridge"*
–New York Times, March 14, 2006

I look at the pile of rubble like so many burned brownies
scraped from a pan to the trash, shards of concrete
and tangled wires, street lights angled into darkness.

.

I remember that bridge, crossing from Biloxi to Ocean Springs,
the wrap-around porch crouching under pre-Katrina live oaks,
reverse mirror of Biloxi's casino-driven urban sprawl.

I think of the miniature sink in the Ocean Springs house,
salvaged from an old passenger train, where I washed out
my traveling undies, the satisfaction in having that sink

all to myself, no sharing with other passengers, Kansas City
to Santa Fe, Birmingham to New Orleans. Rebuilding
the bridge plays itself in other memories–mother's cousins

chopping up their grandmother's organ for firewood,
an organ whose bellows were worn, no longer able
to create a vacuum, or my grandfather's roll top desk

sold when he moved to our small house, room barely large
enough for his bed, never mind his newspaper archives.
I think of my great-aunt's stereoscope and the dual images

miraculously three-dimensional to my six-year-old
pleasure, and I wonder where they are. Perhaps they
were thrown out with my grandmother's davenport,

her enameled pie safe, and her wide gold wedding ring,
or sold at auction with my first Kodak, my silver
clarinet, and my father's collection of glass swans.

**Pitch the Ball Already!**

> *Every pitch was a matter of life and death...*
> *—Joshua Ferris,* To Rise Again at a Decent Hour

Burtville was my introduction to baseball, its dirt diamond hidden
in the pasture behind the country store on the road to nowhere.

Crawling along the gravel roads like so many ants to honey,
cars found those bush-league games just after Sunday dinner.

Fans sitting on fenders drank Coca-Cola and cheered strike-outs
and homeruns indiscriminately. The game meant little to me.

But I had ripened twelve-year-old lust for the red baseball caps worn
by the older girls, eyes on the muscles rippling above the bats.

The blood-red connection spidering between player and fan,
a bare hint of the web of dalliance woven into backwoods life.

I knew little then of balls pitched or caught in the deep pockets
of well-oiled gloves, the thrust of the bat, the legs rounding third.

## Figurative Geometry

> *...the circle–antithesis of the line.*
> *–Richard Flanagan, The Narrow Road to the Deep North*

Images of continuation, circle and line mark
    two very different states of mind. I used to think
        that I was moving inextricably beyond

the hills of Missouri that trapped me in their rise and fall
    their determined movement from point A to B
        as though life could be measured

by the wooden ruler with its embedded metal line.
    Progress, I was told, by my entrepreneurial father
        standing firmly on the courthouse square,

wingtips gleaming from a Kiwi buff, was a matter of will, optimistic
    determination to move onward in an unswerving line
        to material success. From job to job, he bettered

his prospects as he turned his sales pitch from cars to insurance
    to real estate. Selling his own home after home as though they
        were merely models his wife had decorated

for the upwardly mobile masses moving from town to country,
    he never knew that he was selling more than the place
        where he ate his roast and hung his coat.

He's going nowhere now in his plaid jacket, decayed threads
    in a vault of steel, guaranteed to protect the Rotarian pin
        in what was once a lapel. And I? Wishing to curve

that Euclidian line, give breadth to its depth, find that I've bent
    too far. Passing the square, I've unintentionally rounded
        my edges, circled back to where I've begun.

I see the distant plot next to his, measured in lines carefully squared
    to hold another vault that simply proves that a different life
        is yet the same, an unexpected, antithetical arc.

## The Hat in the Frame

*We are our stories. We tell them to stay alive or keep alive*
*those who only live now in the telling.*
*—Niall Williams, History of the Rain*

I never knew my mother's father.
He remains a figment of imagination,
of half truths kerned between stray comments
and the smudged photo in the black frame.

I peer at the black overcoat and see
that it's not as severe as I had thought.
Coat and legend merge in mother's
resistance to his rigid creedal zeal.

No Santa for her, no tree or tinsel
to soften the harsh Missouri winters
or the judgmental moustache, bushy
beneath penetrating eyes, grim mouth.

I reach back in time and place the red
on white Baby Ruth in her grubby hand.

## Zugunruhe

*"It's Time to Discuss Migration, but I've Got to Be Moving On"*
*–The New York Times, April 4, 2006*

The stonechats of Africa, unlike their European cousins,
have no genetic predisposition to migrate
but they do share *zugunruhe,* the nocturnal restlessness
that causes their migratory relatives to take flight.
When *zugunruhe* comes, these African stonechats,
fluttering about all night long, must wonder at the urge
they feel, their inability to settle on just the right limb,
to get a restful night's sleep. No doubt they know
they will be short-tempered next day, grumbling

when fat flies exceed their grasp, their black heads
shaking in disbelief, chestnut breasts swelling
with indignation. Sedentary soul that I am,
I too experience *zugunruhe,* tossing and turning,
my sheets snarled in a web that traps my body
as stray thoughts, residue of unfinished daily
business, trap my mind. I hatch elaborate plans,
solve problems that are barely problems,
and write poems unremembered when the light

of morning finally comes. Vague unrest
lingers and I second-guess choices made,
wonder if Missouri wouldn't have been better
than the swamps of Louisiana, wonder whether
I would have been happier as a veterinarian
than a teacher, wonder if I should have married
that Missouri farmer, the determined jaw, black
hair parted severely in the middle of his head.
I browse job listings, consider updating my resume,

think of applying for a Fulbright. Foregoing lunch
I drive to Kincaid Lake, think idly of remodeling
a shabby cabin with a For Sale sign in overgrown
weeds. Visualizing the butterscotch paint
for roughened walls, I spot a speckled brown
snake entering a hole just under the eaves.
I drive on, circle the lake back to town,
the staid mediocrity of my subdivision,
and decide to mow my lawn, plant petunias.

## Night Is Made for Birth

Walking the measured incline in the blackness of the night,
strange shadows cast by the single outdoor light,
the crisp air nudging the memory of my warm bed,
we approached the red barn, newly built to shelter sheep,
provide a nursery safe as a stable for a king. My mother,

resolute, sure-footed, yet anxious at having to rouse
my twelve-year-old body from dreams of spelling bees,
long division, and the valentine box I'd worked late
to decorate, crepe paper and carefully cut hearts. I stumbled
to keep her gait only dimly aware of my feet striking

the frozen ground, booted loafers crammed in wool socks
bearing no resemblance to the breathing warmth we approached.
Wool-clad bodies nosed the lespedeza, dozed beside sleeping lambs,
bleated softly as we entered the steamy warmth, the pungent smell
of sheep reaching deep into our nostrils. Our lantern sought

the restless movement in the herd. The ewe darted in and out
of drowsy sheep, oblivious to her plight, breech-birthed legs
swinging from her uncontrolled buttocks. My father, distanced
by his night job, my mother alone, the midwife of the flock,
had been in and out of this barn most nights of the week

while I slept in the deep feather bed insensitive
to the push and pull of life beyond my dreams. This time
the task was beyond my mother's strength to cope,
the frenetic woolen sister repudiating her healing
hands. The ewe's head buried in the warmth of my belly,

my arms encircling her nubby body, I became one
with her struggle while my mother eased the new-born
lamb, wiped its startled face and nudged life into its form.
Sweat rolled down my back and the beat of the mother's heart
seemed mine. Toweled dry, the stumbling lamb found
its mother's welcome tit, its tail pinwheeled my excitement.

## Maneuvers

The children drew bombs on the margins
       of their Big Chief tablets,
embossed their second-grade cursive
       with biplanes and jeeps.
Tracks of tanks rolled over the words
       of blameless primers.

They planted their victory gardens
       with the innocence of the poppies
of Flanders fields, and dug foxholes
       in their backyards to protect
puppies and kittens from the Germans
       suspected to live one block over.

War was remote, a star peeping from lace
       curtaining a darkened window.
Distance created a romantic haze
       that not even Nagasaki's cloud
penetrated as voices pledged the flag
       and sang of star-spangled reality.

## One Poet's Hymn

God, you made it look so easy
when you wrote
your first story in the void of words.
No writer's block there,
no cuneiform, only pure metrics
of divine chirography.
The oeuvre of a master
left on the table for redaction.

Letter by letter, we shift and spin,
trying desperately to make sense
of our confounded Babel. Struggling
to put our marks on a gyrating
dance of flesh becoming,
we flounder like so many netted
fish fed to ravenous multitudes.

Our greedy, word mongering fingers
continue to reach for the gift
of syllables joined, runes crafted
in the mystery of being
we barely grasp in shaky strokes.
Ours, the gratuity of language,
the sheer joy of word on word,
the Alpha and Omega of voice.

**Forgiveness**

Dead men walk over the fingers
of God's holy hand, counting
knuckles and nails, careful
to note the wrinkled skin.

They seek the upturned palm
to snuggle like so many kittens
in a basket of yarn, seeking
always seeking, warm suckle.

They dare not challenge
the opposable thumb, but lean
into the fingered dexterity
that made them once whole.

## Table Talk

The bread was porous
        like a sponge.
It sucked the wine
        from the chalice
held out in compassion
        taken in hate.

Kneeling like a stick figure
        contorted by childish
crayon tracks on rough paper,
        his plastic contrition
was as savage as primitive
        drawings on a cave wall.

Chewing the morsels of the body
        was sheer cannibalism,
a rejection of life, the denial
        of brotherhood. It signaled
the depths of his own heresy,
        his utter alienation.

Swallowing was like force-feeding
        a comatose patient, the tube
scratching the larynx as it descended
        through a recalcitrant trachea,
the breath of the body of Christ unable
        to penetrate bronchial blockage.

The darkness was the forced burial
        of a cataclysmic mudslide,
rapid, unforeseen, devastating.
        Prayers, murmuring distant
pleas, seemed both his and not his,
        grace, a single heartbeat.

A Methodist pastor, a retired English professor, editor, clarinetist, and poet, Rosanne Osborne holds the Ph.D. in English from the University of Alabama, the MFA from Spalding University, and the MRE and MDiv from New Orleans Baptist Theological Seminary. She grew up in Missouri, but she has lived most of her adult life in Louisiana. She taught for 39 years at Louisiana College, a small liberal arts college in Pineville, Louisiana, and she was editor of Royal Service, a missions magazine for Baptist Women for five years in the latter sixties and early seventies in Birmingham, Alabama. She is currently pastor of First United Methodist Church in Oakdale. Louisiana. Her work has appeared in Tar River Poetry, Alabama Review, Christian Century, Ruminate, Thema, Penwood Review, The Village Pariah, and several other journals. Tapestry of Counterpoint is her first collection of poems.

Her mother was a quilter, so she inherited an affinity for scraps. Odd-shaped pieces from the dressmaker's floor, a diversity of fabrics from her dad's old pants and coats, patches cut from the feed-sacks of chicken mash bought when the family went to town on Saturdays–their patterns imprinted her psyche with a reverence for incongruity and associational reasoning–an over-riding sense of counterpoint.

The subjects chosen for her poems have that same eclectic range as the patterns of her childhood. From the ruminations of memory to notions gleaned from avid reading of fiction and nonfiction, from observations in nature to preoccupations with questions, sounds, and sights, her poems are simply a celebration of the past and the present years of her life.

www.ingramcontent.com/pod-product-compliance
Lightning Source LLC
Chambersburg PA
CBHW022046080426
42734CB00009B/1253